12

Hiro Mashima

Translated and adapted by William Flanagan
Lettered by North Market Street Graphics

W9-AOI-213

Ballantine Books · New York

Fairy Tail volume 12 is a work of fiction. Names, characters, places, and incidents are the products of the author's imagination or are used fictitiously. Any resemblance to actual events, locales, or persons, living or dead, is entirely coincidental.

A Del Rey Manga/Kodansha Trade Paperback Original

Fairy Tail volume 12 copyright © 2008 Hiro Mashima
English translation copyright © 2010 Hiro Mashima

All rights reserved.

Published in the United States by Del Rey, an imprint of The Random House Publishing Group, a division of Random House, Inc., New York.

DEL REY is a registered trademark and the Del Rey colophon is a trademark of Random House, Inc.

Publication rights arranged through Kodansha Ltd.

First published in Japan in 2008 by Kodansha Ltd., Tokyo

ISBN 978-0-345-51993-1

Printed in the United States of America

www.delreymanga.com

9 8 7 6 5 4 3 2 1

Translator/Adapter: William Flanagan
Lettering: North Market Street Graphics

Contents

I went to a signing in San Diego, USA! Uwooh!!
I was a little worried. What would I do if I went to the signing and nobody showed up? But my fears were groundless—a huge group of people were there, and the signing was a smashing success!! (Phew! That was a relief!) This is a picture of me going on a rampage when some nice fan gave me a scarf just like Natsu's!

—Hiro Mashima

Honorifics Explained

Throughout the Del Rey Manga books, you will find Japanese honorifics left intact in the translations. For those not familiar with how the Japanese use honorifics and, more important, how they differ from American honorifics, we present this brief overview.

Politeness has always been a critical facet of Japanese culture. Ever since the feudal era, when Japan was a highly stratified society, use of honorifics—which can be defined as polite speech that indicates relationship or status—has played an essential role in the Japanese language. When addressing someone in Japanese, an honorific usually takes the form of a suffix attached to one's name (example: "Asuna-san"), is used as a title at the end of one's name, or appears in place of the name itself (example: "Negi-sensei," or simply "Sensei").

Honorifics can be expressions of respect or endearment. In the context of manga and anime, honorifics give insight into the nature of the relationship between characters. Many English translations leave out these important honorifics and therefore distort the feel of the original Japanese. Because Japanese honorifics contain nuances that English honorifics lack, it is our policy at Del Rey not to translate them. Here, instead, is a guide to some of the honorifics you may encounter in Del Rey Manga.

-san: This is the most common honorific and is equivalent to Mr., Miss, Ms., or Mrs. It is the all-purpose honorific and can be used in any situation where politeness is required.

-sama: This is one level higher than "-san" and is used to confer great respect.

-dono: This comes from the word "tono," which means "lord." It is an even higher level than "-sama" and confers utmost respect.

-kun: This suffix is used at the end of boys' names to express familiarity or endearment. It is also sometimes used by men among friends, or when addressing someone younger or of a lower station.

-chan: This is used to express endearment, mostly toward girls. It is also used for little boys, pets, and even between lovers. It gives a sense of childish cuteness.

Bozu: This is an informal way to refer to a boy, similar to the English terms "kid" and "squirt."

**Sempai/
Senpai:** This title suggests that the addressee is one's senior in a group or organization. It is most often used in a school setting, where underclassmen refer to their upperclassmen as "sempai." It can also be used in the workplace, such as when a newer employee addresses an employee who has seniority in the company.

Kohai: This is the opposite of "sempai" and is used toward underclassmen in school or newcomers in the workplace. It connotes that the addressee is of a lower station.

Sensei: Literally meaning "one who has come before," this title is used for teachers, doctors, or masters of any profession or art.

-[blank]: This is usually forgotten in these lists, but it is perhaps the most significant difference between Japanese and English. The lack of honorific means that the speaker has permission to address the person in a very intimate way. Usually, only family, spouses, or very close friends have this kind of permission. Known as *yobisute*, it can be gratifying when someone who has earned the intimacy starts to call one by one's name without an honorific. But when that intimacy hasn't been earned, it can be very insulting.

CONTENTS

Chapter 92: Destiny

SLISS

In fifteen minutes...

!!

However, you will lose too... to Jellal...

L-Lost. That is...the first time...that has happened... since I entered the guild...

SLUMP

Ah... That poem was terrible...

Fall down upon us; O light of divine justice; Bring death to us all!

Quickly, gather up Simon and the others, along with my friends from the guild, and get as far away from here as you can!

!

Shô, you're wounded. Can you walk?

Y-Yeah... I think so...

Fifteen minutes?

Is she talking about Etherion?

9

You will do as I ask, won't you...

...Shô?

B-But...

What about you, sis?

TMP ひた
ひた
ひた TMP

Yeah.

I'll meet you, but first...

...I'm going to end this!

Huh?

Wha—?!!

So you're awake, Natsu?

Stop that!!! Don't get sick just remembering!!!

URP!

UWOOO...

I was riding on this weird moving vehicle...

That cat flew him from the tower.

But Gray was pretty beaten up in the battle too.

After that, you were eaten by Fukuro and saved by Gray.

By Gray?!!

Hey! Focus!!

I just know he's going to use this against me for a whole month!!! He's the kind of guy who never knows when a joke gets old!

DAMMIT!

I don't know if I'd call it "losing." You were eaten.

Arrrgg!!! It isn't possible!!! How can I lose and Gray win?!!!

This isn't the time for stunts like that!!!!

GWIP

I can't let this stand!!!! I need revenge!!!! I'm going off to fight that dumb Fukuro again!!!!

This time, I'll do it with an arm tied behind my back!!!! If I have a handicap like that, then—

GURK!

I'm Simon. Erza's old friend.

By the way, who are you again?

D-Don't worry about me... Just listen, Natsu...

SLUMP

Hey, are you hurt?!

They didn't understand the situation, but with some persuasion, I got them to take your friends out of the tower.

Myaa! Simon says they're allies now!

Weren't these guys supposed to be enemies?

ZGGL
ZGGL

A little while ago, I got a message from Wally and Millia.

They found Lucy, Juvia, and one of the Trinity Raven passed out in a hall.

She said she was going to finish all of this.

The only one left is Jellal, and Erza is going after him.

But I didn't beat any of them!!!

Soon after, I got a message from Shô saying that all three of the Trinity Raven have been defeated.

...but Jellal is much too powerful...

A fight to the death may be an unavoidable destiny for them... Fate has bound those two for eight years.

!!!?
...

I don't wanna!

So please!!! Go rescue Erza!!!

KALUNK

Is it really so fun to play games with people's lives?

SST

Well, it looks like the game is almost over.

ROLL ROLL

KLUNK

Or to put it another way, life on its own is boring and empty.

Within the balance of life and death is the origin and sum of all emotions.

"Fun"? Yes, it is.

You could have escaped whenever you felt like it, you know.

Take them. I don't need them anymore.

The Tower of Heaven is complete!

I'm here to free my former friends.

FSSH

No... Etherion will fall.

You're too relaxed. It was a trick after all, wasn't it?

GRIMP

You mean Etherion?

HEH HEH...

Even if it will be destroyed in ten minutes?

You... refuse to save your friend...?

Refuse to rescue Erza?!!

He's Erza's enemy. Erza can finish him off herself.

This isn't a problem I can go sticking my nose in.

Who do you think Erza is, you jerk?!!!!

Erza can never beat Jellal!!!!

FSHH

Jellal's a cunning plotter.

He's going to use that against her.

Of course if that comes down, nothing will be left of this tower and everyone in it!

And the situation is even worse than that.

Did you know that the Magic Council is about to bring Etherion down on our heads?

You know Erza pretty well, don't you? I don't want to believe it, but...

...I think she may be going in order to make sure that Jellal dies in the Etherion blast, along with herself.

Erza told everyone to try to escape, then she went off alone.

What?!!

According to Shô, it'll hit us in fifteen— No, now it's more like ten minutes!

Why didn't you say that first?!!

GRND GRND

FAIRY TAIL

Chapter 93: Pray to the Sacred Light

So what is your real purpose behind all this?

Kh!

It's true the principles and construction would be exactly as it was in the plans...

...but there was one very important element missing.

You didn't think I'd spend eight years doing nothing, did you?

I did my research on the R-System.

You really haven't finished the R-System, have you?

!!!

What's missing is...

...the magic power!!!

I'm talking about even before the sacrifice!

I already told you about that... The sacrifice was you.

To power such an enormous magical device... ...you will need more than 270 million edea of magic power!!

You could gather every wizard on the continent, and still not be sure you'd have power on that scale.

. . . . .

Not only could one person not do it, but this tower doesn't even have the capacity to store up that much power.

On top of that, you know about the Council's attack, and still you're not trying to escape.

That means you're plotting something!!!

So is it your desire to die here and now?!!!

Jellal!!! Your dream ended a long time ago!!!!

Three minutes until Etherion...

If that's it, then we're both going together!!!!

I'm going to hold you down here with my own hands until the final moment!!!!

Urn...

Kh...

That isn't such a bad idea...

A- All right...

I'm just a puppet he uses until he can revive his own flesh.

Zeref's spirit took over my body...

And he doesn't listen to me...

I couldn't save myself...

I couldn't save any of my friends...

"Took over"?

All of existence was finished before it ever even started.

There is no heaven.

Look where you want, you'll never find freedom either.

The final phase of the Etherion launch is complete!

Deploy the Satellite Square!!!

Our prayers go with it.

Our prayers go with it.

Our prayers go with it.

Our prayers go with it.

Natsu...
Erza...

Hurry up and get out of there...

Wait a second! Was the Council serious about sending down Etherion?!!

Myaa!

There's no way I could have been able to finish the R-System...

...but Zeref's spirit wouldn't allow me to let up.

Erza...

I'm just a broken engine that he's driving.

No one...is able to stop him now.

That's why you came here, isn't it?

You win.

Kill me.

FWOOOOON

It's all over.

For you...

...and for me too.

KLAKK

SST

I don't have to do anything. You hear that screech, right?

The Satellite Square has been deployed, targeting this tower.

So you're just another of Zeref's victims?

You always were a clumsy person, huh?

Chapter 94: One Person

Etherion...

Was the attack a success?!! Get me confirmation fast!!!

I repeat, Etherion struck right on target!!!

Etherion was directly on target!!!

Era...

The density of Ethernano fusion is increasing!

We predict extreme weather conditions!

It's impossible to avoid a few sacrifices when we need to stop that.

They were organized with the purpose of reviving Zeref.

I wonder how many people were in that tower.

...that won't alleviate the loss to families of those sacrificed.

What-ever our justifica-tions...

Natsu...

Erza...

...and the interior was... crystal?

The outer walls have all crumbled away...

...is that...?

Wh-What...

Natsu and Erza...and that guy Simon...?

Say... They're okay, right?

What happened to this place... and what's it changed into?

Oww...

Etherion fell...

Wh-Why am I still...

AH HA HA HA HA

Finally!!!!

Finally the time has come!!!!

Does this surprise you, Erza?

Heh heh heh...

You...

And because of the Council and Etherion...

This is the true form of the Tower of Heaven!!

It is a giant lacrima crystal!!

You were so cute, Erza!

S-So that was all a trick, huh...?

Eh?!

Wh-What are you doing here?!!

Still... since we have exactly the same face, it's only natural.

You mistook me for Jellal and attacked.

I remember the first time we met, Erza.

You came to turn in case reports to the Council with Makarov.

But your hostility never abated.

HYUUOOOOOOO

ヒョォォォォ

You finally were talked down when I told you we were twins.

At the time I should have said something that would have convinced you that I was going to find Jellal and kill him.

Ah, yes. That was a mistake of mine.

Even worse... you were spying on me for him!!!

What did you expect?!! You spent all your time covering up what Jellal was doing rather than stopping him as a brother should!!!

So you two...were in collusion all along, huh?

There's nothing more painful than those excuses made up on the spot, is there?

But my biggest mistake was to encounter you at all, right after becoming a member of the Council.

"Collusion"? That isn't quite the right word.

He vanished...

Sieg... just disappeared!

Exactly!

Sieg is me.

Thought projection?!!!

I-If that's the case, then you dropped Etherion down on your own head!!!

Is that the whole reason you wormed your way onto the Council?!!

I don't believe it!!!

Of course that and everything else was all a part of Zeref's plan to be revived.

Was your transient freedom enjoyable, Erza?

Chapter 95:
Sleeping Beauty Warrior

No. I should say, for the sake of Jellal-sama!

It's all for Sieg-sama...

Ultear!!

Here and now is when...

...his dream becomes a reality!!!

That's the real form of the R-System that we helped to build.

It's started up!!

What?!!

It's the R-System!!

I don't know... It's the first time that we've seen it started up too.

Started up, you say?!!

You don't mean they're reviving Zeref, do you?!!

Where is that might you showed a little while ago?

ZUSHAAA

Unff!!

Did you use up all your magical power fighting with Ikaruga?

WHOOSH

GRMMM

GRN
GRN
GRN
ギ!!...

Urk!

My body...

...refuses to move!!!

KRANG

CLANK

GRRRRN

Ah!!

Urg!!

Ahhh!!!

So all that's left is the human sacrifice, and I can revive Zeref.

I now have enough magical power to use the R-System.

And it will break down your body into its smallest components only to reform as Zeref's body.

That 270 million edea of magical power stored in the lacrima will fuse with your body.

I'm afraid I have no time left to play with you, Erza.

Jellal...

Jellal
!!!!

Really ?!

F-Forgive me... My body... can't move...

Natsu... You have to get out of here now...

HA HA HA HAAA!!!

S-Stop it...

You're always giving me beatings I can never forget!! Well take this!!!

TICKLE TICKLE TICKLE TICKLE TICKLE

You don't know who you're fighting...

You don't know enough about him to beat him!!!

I don't wanna! If you don't want to do it yourself, I'll do the fighting for you!

No...!

76

Please...

BLUP

Do what I say...

You're saying that if I don't know, I can't win?

Yo!

Wh-What are you...

GWMM

Eh?

Erza, I don't know enough about you either.

WHUDD

ZLIFF

. . . . . .

Are you happy now that you hurt an opponent that couldn't move?

You're even more outrageous than the rumors say.

... was crying.

Erza...

I don't ever want to see Erza like that!!!

She spit out her words in that weak whisper, and her voice was quavering.

She's at her best when she's strong and violent!!!

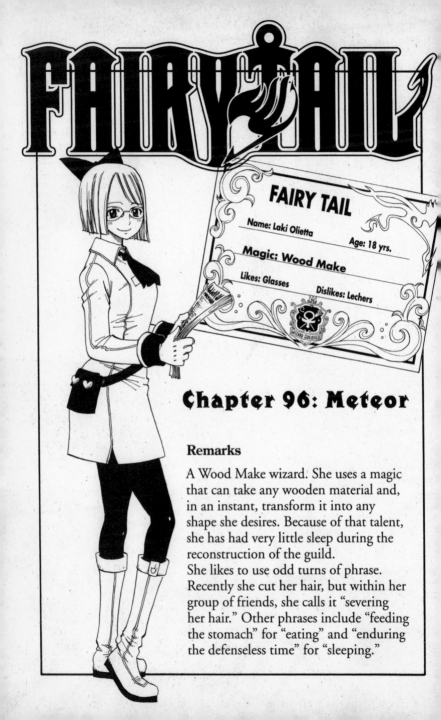

FAIRY TAIL

Name: Laki Olietta

Age: 18 yrs.

Magic: Wood Make

Likes: Glasses

Dislikes: Lechers

Chapter 96: Meteor

Remarks

A Wood Make wizard. She uses a magic that can take any wooden material and, in an instant, transform it into any shape she desires. Because of that talent, she has had very little sleep during the reconstruction of the guild.

She likes to use odd turns of phrase. Recently she cut her hair, but within her group of friends, she calls it "severing her hair." Other phrases include "feeding the stomach" for "eating" and "enduring the defenseless time" for "sleeping."

I felt a desire to have a taste of a dragon slayer's attack before I personally wiped them off the face of the Earth.

POFF
POFF

What was that? !!!

If that's all you can do, then you lack substance for the awe you inspire.

For that, I think I'll turn you into fodder for my *heavenly body* magic.

But you did interfere with my ritual.

CHASSH

CRETCH!

HGRUUN

WHUDD

This kind of destruction magic is like being hit by a falling meteor.

It's amazing your body is still in one piece.

The magical power is already starting to leak out.

If the R-System takes any more damage, it wouldn't be good.

But I must say that I may have overdone it a bit.

Mustn't we, Erza?

We must hurry.

!

TONK

TONK

KLAK

TONK

ROLL

Heh heh...

...my attack...

...it struck you...

THUNK

Then this is not your lucky day!!!!

Don't do that!!!!

GOO

OOM

This tower... This crystal? You just said damage wouldn't be good for it, right...?

GRRNN

...of everybody in Fairy Tail.

Breaking things is a specialty...

FAIRY TAIL

Chapter 97:
A Life as a Shield

I'm going to finish you in an instant!!

You'll regret standing up to me when you're on your way to hell!!!

One thing I know about me is that I can take punishment.

So if you can take me down, go ahead and try!!!

!!!

DOGOOOOM

...Kôen
!!!!*

*Fire Dragon's Gleeming Flame.

He's...
targeting
the
tower...

SKRRRRRCH

は゛ッ

!!!

Do you dare kill me?!!!

Zeref needs a sacrifice to be revived, right?!!

But now that it comes to this, it doesn't have to be you!!!

Yes...One condition is that the body be of a wizard that is fit to be a wizard saint.

Erza!!! Get out of the way!!!

Bow to your death!!!

Both of you together...

!!

You have nothing to worry about!!!

I will protect you!!!

...Altairis!!!!

heavenly body magic...

No!!! Don't!!!!

DOO

OOM

SLUMP

...za...

Er...

Simon...

Was that bug still crawling around this place?

THUDD

Simon!!!

Why didn't you...

...escape like the others?!!

| | |

I knew... that someday...

...that I... ...help... ...you...

AFF!

FF...!

I-I'm... glad...

HAHH HAHH

Simon !!!

HAHH

HAHH

You... were... always so... sweet...

...so nice...

HAHH

HAHH

Okay, I understand!!! Now don't try to speak anymore!!!

I've always...

...loved you...

Simon...

: : :

HAHH HAHH

!!

THUNK

Nooooooooo !!!!!

AH HA HA HA HA HA

The most pitiful thing I've ever seen!!!!

How pitiful !!!

TWITCH

Simon !!!!

They call that "death without meaning" !!!

This changes absolutely nothing!!! No matter what you do, nobody is leaving this tower alive!!!

Chapter 98:
Dragon Force

What are you doing this for?!! It's stupid!!!

Ethernanos are fused with all sorts of power, not just flame!!!

GAH-HAHH!!!

GURK

GURK

What?! Does he think he can power up with any magical power, even if it isn't fire?

GAHH!!

GWAHHH!!!

Natsu!!!

AAAAAAA

AAAAA

With messed-up logic like that, he'll finish himself off for me!!

What?!!

A dragon!!

That's right... I'm the only one who can feel Zeref!!!

He quietly asked me if I wanted true freedom!!!

In my fear and pain, Zeref whispered to me!!!

Together with Zeref, I will create a nation of true freedom!!!!

I am the chosen one!!!!

And you tried to make it by stealing the freedom of everybody else!!!!

Why don't you stupid people understand that?!!!

Only those with the will to change the world have the ability to alter history!!!

All I need is another eight years... No, I can complete it in five...

Zeref... just you wait!!!

Is he going to destroy everything, including the tower?!!!

Is that an Abyss Break?!!!

Kh...

!!!

ZHAAN

ZLATZ

!!!

You won't ever get your freedom!!!!

No jerk whose will is controlled by ghosts can ever find freedom!!!!

CHASSH

GWOOM

DOO

OOM

Is this
Natsu's
true
power...?

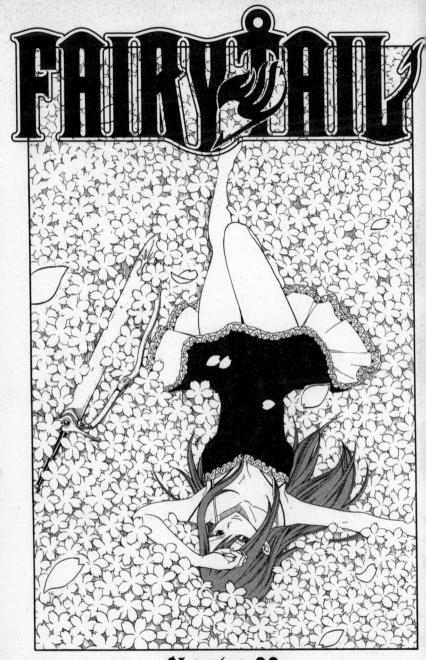

Chapter 99:
Titania Falls

He defeated as powerful a man as Jellal...

My fight, a fight that's been going on for eight years, is over.

!!

And now... my friends can find true freedom...

Natsu
!!!

You really are amazing

Truly!

I-It couldn't be that Etherion has gone on a rampage, could it?!!

What is that?!!

The tower...!!!

Basically anything trying to contain that much magical power in one place would be unstable...

On a rampage?!!

What about my sis and the others inside?!!

Wait a second!! With us this close, we're going to—

It's bursting out and causing an explosion...

It's a tidal wave of magical power with no place to go...

We're in danger here...

There's something more urgent than who can be rescued and who can't...

GWOO

DOOM

...of complete destruction!!!

KREMBL

ZUSHAAA

Umphh...

With things as they are, even if we get outside the building, we'll still be caught up in the blast!!!

It looks to have a lot more destructive power than I ever imagined!!!

This magic power is warping its container... the lacrima crystal...

BA

Dammit !!!

Does it all end here?!!

No...

When did I ever give up?!!

This time, it's my turn to rescue you...

...Natsu!!!

So what do I do...?!!

But it's impossible to contain the blast or even escape...

"Fuse"?

"That 270 million edea of magical power stored in the lacrima will fuse with your body."

"And it will break down your body into its smallest components only to reform as Zeref's body."

I'll just have to risk it!!!!

...then the power will use my body as its container and I can stop the explosion.

If I can fuse with the Etherion energy...

Good!!! The lacrima crystal is allowing my body inside!!!

Errnn...

ZUPUMM

Arrg!!!

Natsu?!!

Erza...

This is the only way to stop Etherion.

What... are you doing...?

Your... body is going into the—

GOCHAAA

GWOO

Stop Etherion...?

Don't be stupid!!! If you do that, you'll—!!!

But if I can fuse with Etherion, I may be able to quiet the energies...

Pretty soon, Etherion will go rampaging, and destroy the tower in a huge explosion.

Uwaah!!!

ZLMM
ZLMM
ZLMM

ZLMM
ZLMM

Stop it!!! Erza!!!

Aaa ah!!!

ZLMM
ZLMM
ZLMM

SKRRCH

GMP.

Erza!!!

Don't worry! I'll figure out a way to quiet it...

Natsu...

Don't do it!!!

FAIRY TAIL

Chapter 100: To Tomorrow

Where am I?!!

No, that isn't it... This place is far more warm...

Inside Etherion?!

!

Oh!

Erza Scarlet

Rest in peace

Am...

Am I
dead?

This woman... Erza Scarlet...

...was loved by the gods, and she loved them.

And she loved us, her friends, as well.

She moved in the way fairies dance, and she was lovelier than the finest scenery nature can produce.

Her heart was as big and limitless as the sky.

Her sword glistened nobly, and was used only for those she loved.

ERZA SCARLET

It is love that makes one strong!

But what makes one weak is also love.

And I...

SNIFF

SNIFF

SNIFF...

...I loved her as a true member of my family...

SNIFF SNIFF

SNIFF SNIFF SNIFF

Master...

...for the peaceful repose of her soul...

I pray...

The Council, in a unanimous decision, with a single empty seat...

...have taken up a resolution to honor this person.

FASSH

These are a waste!!!

Stop that now, Natsu!!!!

Natsu...

Erza isn't dead!!!

You jerk!!

Natsu, don't...

Wake up to reality, for pity's sake!!!!

She can't be dead, right?!!!

Please, Natsu... Don't!

Erza's still alive !!!!

Let go of me !!!!

CLAMMER

CLAMMER

CLAMMER

But...

GAN

NCH

I did it... for Natsu's future...

Is this the future of everyone left behind?

Is this their future?

I just did it so that everybody could smile again...

I didn't want to see a future like this!!

I'm begging you... Please stop crying like that...

I can't...

Make it stop!

I can't do this...

It's so wonderful that you're all right!!!!

What did you have to go worrying us like that for?!!

What... happened here?

Sis!!!!

Am I...

...alive?

But... how...?

Natsu...

You saved me?

Could he have found me inside that huge tornado of magic power...?

Wh-What kind of man can do that...?

It's the same for me.

Eh?

SLUMP

SPAA

AASH

It's the same for all of us...

"If it weren't for Fairy Tail, I wouldn't have been able to go on."

"I can't even imagine life without my friends."

Don't ever
do that
again...

Never again !!!!

Natsu...

HIK...

SNIFF SNIFF

Mira: Next question!

If Shô was stuck in the tower all that time, why is he so suntanned!?

 : There it is!! The question that points out problems with the whole setup!!

 : The answer must be that he wasn't inside the tower for that entire time.

Lucy: You...think so?

Mira: He made it all the way to the hotel on Akane Beach, right? He must have had a little bit of freedom.

Lucy: I got it!! Shô-kun was the only one allowed to work on the tower's walls!! That's why he's so tanned!

 : All right!! We've solved it!!

: "Solved it"? I just made a wild guess and threw it out for consideration...

Mira: With that, we come to the final question!

What the heck is a Unison Raid!?

Lucy: I don't really know myself. It just happened by coincidence at the time...If we were asked to do it again, I don't think we could.

Mira: A Unison Raid is what it sounds like. It's an attack where two different types of magic become one, raising the attack level to one much higher than it would be if both were cast at the same enemy separately.

Lucy: Wooow!! I did something really incredible, didn't I?

 : They say that for all the recorded Unison Raids up to now, it could only happen between two friends so close they could almost read each other's thoughts. And even then, it's difficult.

Lucy: "Friends"...huh? Well, we can't claim that, but at the time...I'm sure that we really accepted each other on a very deep level, huh?

 : No, it was simply coincidence! Stomp, stomp, stomp....

: ....

: After you went and said something that sounded cool.

Lucy: ....

Mira: Oh, dear! What is the matter? Lucy's frozen up like a statue!

Lucy: ....

 : Okay, everybody! See you in the next volume!! Moun•tain•li•on•poooon!!!

 : Hey!! That's my line!!!

Emergency Request
Explain the Mysteries of...
FAIRY TAIL!?

From the Counter at Fairy Tail...

 : Moun·tain·li·on·poooon!!!

 : What's that supposed to be?

Lucy: I thought the phrase would catch on. You know, something to get the people energized! *Moun·tain·li·on·poooon!!!*

Mira: You know, I really doubt it's going to catch on.

Lucy: You're probably right.

Mira: And...straight to the first question.

That scar on Natsu's neck... What's it from?

Lucy: We get this question a lot!

Mira: That's true...I think it's the most common question.

Lucy: But I've got to say that I'm amazed at how observant some people are!

Mira: What amazes me is with all those letters, we're only getting around to it now...

 : It's probably because the author hasn't thought up the answer yet, right?

 : That certainly is one possibility...

Lucy: Eh? What? You're saying that there's some big secret behind it?

Mira: Anyway, the editor put in a word of advice on this, and taking that advice to heart, this matter is a S·e·c·r·e·t! ♡

 : I get the feeling that we didn't do anything to answer the question...

Lucy: So, on to the next question.

Those suits of Erza's armor that were cut to pieces, are they gone forever? I really loved the fire empress armor...

Lucy: The fire empress armor. It certainly is popular, isn't it?

Mira: Of course! It's Erza in twin ponytails!

Lucy: And the extremely high leg lines.

Mira: If she sends it out for repairs, she can get it fixed, right?

Lucy: Is *that* your answer?!!

Continued on the right-hand page.

TAIL D'ART

The *Fairy Tail* Guild d'Art is an explosion of fan art! Please send in your black-and-white art!! Those chosen to be published will get a signed mini poster! ♪ Make sure you write your real name and address on the back of your postcard!

▲ You realize that Ikaruga is the name of a bird, right? Fukuro (Owl) and Taka (Hawk) are just as their names say.

Kumamoto Prefecture, Hideyo Noguchi

▲ Whoa! Was Elfman ever looking this cool?!

Gunma Prefecture, STM

▲ This is a really great smile on Natsu!! Just between you and me, Natsu's eyes are a little more catlike than most of the other characters.

Kagoshima Prefecture, Mai Nishimura

▲ Uwa ha ha ha!! This is incredibly good!! What is it? What makes it so cute?!!

Fukushima Prefecture, Erumo

▲ Oohh!! If I ever actually come across a scene like this, I may be forced to do whatever the person wants.

Tôyama Prefecture, Tomoyo

▲ Huh? It looks like everybody's paired off into couples...

Saitama Prefecture, Maccha

● Any letters and postcards you send means that your personal information—such as your name, address, postal code, and other information you include—will be handed over, as is, to the author. When you send mail, please keep that in mind.

▲ Uhyooon!! Everybody's in high-school uniforms!! This kind of picture could be turned into a key holder!

Saitama Prefecture, Leona

FAIRY GUILD

Send to

Hiro Mashima c/o Del Rey Manga, 1745 Broadway, New York, NY 10019*
*Del Rey Manga will make every effort to send your letters to the author, but cannot guarantee a response. Do not send original artwork, as it cannot be returned.

► Art from a Mirajane rooter!! You can see her in every Question Corner.

Gifu Prefecture, Yuki Mori

► Loke!! He hasn't had much of a part lately, but he'll show up again!! Watch for him, fans!

Gifu Prefecture, Yuki

► Extremely well done! It's like Lucy's face has a wonderful individuality to it!

Yamaguchi Prefecture,, I♡59

► Everybody pose for the picture!!! You really went for it! Thanks for drawing all of those characters!

Iwate Prefecture, Saaya

► A little Mirajane-chan! This kind of image is pretty rare!

Shizuoka Prefecture, Okara•Y

Re-jec-tion Cor-ner

Gifu Prefecture, Shōgo Hatanaka

D-Did this scene really have that much impact on the readers? Or was this all sent by people in the same family?

IT'S OLD-MAN CRUX'S TIME

NOW!!!

Yamaguchi Prefecture, Kōki Nakagawa

BURY ME IN THE REJECTED WORKS !!

Hokkaido, Zeek

About the Creator

HIRO MASHIMA was born May 3, 1977, in the Nagano prefecture. His series *Rave Master* has made him one of the most popular manga artists in America. *Fairy Tail*, currently being serialized in *Weekly Shōnen Magazine*, is his latest creation.

AFTERWORD

The Erza chapter is over! Thank you for hanging in there!!! No, really, that's how I feel. I hung in, and I'm a little tired. But those last images in the book where Natsu and Erza are hugging—I really wanted to draw that!! I wanted to draw the scene where Erza was crying out of both eyes!! I worked hard through the whole story arc just to get to those. The fact that Erza could only cry out of one eye was something I had decided on at the beginning, and if you look at all the images of her crying, you'll see it foreshadowed in those...But there's one scene where I made a mistake and had tears streaming out of both eyes. (Sweat, sweat.) And I had paid so much attention to foreshadowing this fact too...so why?!! (Did I simply forget?)

Actually, this entire Erza chapter was a parody of my last work, *Rave Master*'s Etherion Chapter. Etherion. Sieg. Sieg's magic. The scene where Natsu is pictured on a black background and his taunts. The fireworks in the next volume too. All that and more were self parodies. Of course, if you don't know about it, it doesn't affect your enjoyment. But I hope those who do know get a small smile on their faces while reading it.

And while concentrating on other things like the above stuff, *Fairy Tail* has reached its one hundredth installment!!! Yaay! I never intended it to go on this long!!! I had thought that I'd stop this series at about ten volumes!! That's what I figured!!! But everybody's warm support got me all fired up!!! Or, to tell you the truth, I just don't think I've drawn enough of the story to finish it off. (Eh-heh!) While I'm in the middle of drawing *Fairy Tail*, I just keep coming up with new things that I want to draw. Even though I haven't even thought through to the next plot twist! (Ha ha.) And so, I'd like to thank you all for your support. I plan to try even harder in the future! In the next volume, we have a character show up again from the old days...(You mean that character's going to be a regular?!!)

199

Translation Notes

Japanese is a tricky language for most Westerners, and translation is often more art than science. For your edification and reading pleasure, here are notes on some of the places where we could have gone in a different direction in our translation of the work, or where a Japanese cultural reference is used.

Names

Hiro Mashima has graciously agreed to provide official English spellings for just about all of the characters in *Fairy Tail*. Because this version of *Fairy Tail* is the first publication of most of these spellings, there will inevitably be differences between these spellings and some of the fan interpretations that may have spread throughout the Web or in other fan circles. Rest assured that what is contained in this book are the spellings that Mashima-sensei wanted for *Fairy Tail*.

General Notes:
Wizard

In the original Japanese version of *Fairy Tail*, there are occasional images where the word "wizard" is found. This translation has taken that as its inspiration, and translated the word *madôshi* as "wizard". But *madôshi's* meaning is similar to certain Japanese words that have been borrowed into the English language, such as judo (the soft way) and kendo (the way of the sword). *Madô* is the way of magic, and *madôshi* are those who follow the way of magic. So although the word "wizard" is used, the Japanese would think less of traditional Western wizards, such as Merlin or Gandalf, and more of martial artists.

San Diego Comic-Con, page iv

The San Diego Comic-Con is America's largest comic-book convention, with an annual attendance of more than 120,000 in the past several years (including 2008, when Mashima-sensei went). Although it was traditionally a convention for American comic books, it has supported anime and manga since the 1980s, and has been a playground for such notable manga luminaries as Monkey Punch (*Lupin III*), Kia Asamiya (*Silent Möbius*), and Rumiko Takahashi (*Inu Yasha*) among many others. In the '90s and especially the decade of the 2000s, movie studios began to see the potential for viral marketing and started to play their previews and host Hollywood stars, directors, and crews in panels plugging their movies. There is even a panel for translators and editors of manga and anime, for any who want to know more about how their favorite manga is brought to English-speaking countries.

Ikaruga's poem, page 9

Ikaruga's poem is a haiku. Haiku is the most popular form of Japanese poetry. A standard haiku verse is a series of seventeen syllables separated into lines of five syllables, then seven, then five. See more about haiku in the notes for volume 11.

Fall down upon us; O light of divine justice; Bring death to us all!

Grand Chariot, page 97

The seven stars Jellal is referring to form the constellation (star cluster) known to most American astronomers and astronomy hobbyists as the Pleiades. However, it is known in French as the Grand Chariot, and although the kanji in Jellal's dialog was written as "Seven Star Sword," the *furigana* pronunciation guide to the kanji reads, "Grand Chariot."

Shaved Ice, page 123

This image depicts a pretty standard summer scene in Japan. Shaved ice is one of the most popular summertime treats for children (and adults) in Japan. It is something like the popular treat, snowcones, in the West, but the amount of toppings is far more varied. Aside from the syrups found in snowcones, shaved ice can also be topped with such things as condensed milk, sweet beans, or maccha green tea.

Moun·tain·li·on·pooon! page 195

What she said in the Japanese was, "Ya·ma·ne·ko·pooon!" which basically means "Mountain Lion·pooon" with the "pooon" part being a meaningless sound intended to make the phrase a little cuter.

TOMARE!

[STOP!]

You're going the wrong way!

Manga is a completely different type of reading experience.

To start at the *beginning*, go to the *end*!

That's right! Authentic manga is read the traditional Japanese way—from right to left, exactly the *opposite* of how American books are read. It's easy to follow: Just go to the other end of the book and read each page—and each panel—from right side to left side, starting at the top right. Now you're experiencing manga as it was meant to be!